THE RIPPLING EFFECT

GRATITUDE TO ME

AARNA KHATRI

Made with ♥ on the Notion Press Platform
www.notionpress.com

The Kindness Foundation is a non-profit and kindness movement that is dedicated to promoting kindness, empathy, and compassion as the pillars of a better world. We run several programs, workshops and events year-round to not only inspire kindness in daily life but also create positive change.

The International Kindness Festival (IKF) is the first of its' kind global celebration of kindness. It is a platform where we share ideas, stories, and experiences that illuminate the path toward a world steeped in kindness.

We strongly believe that it is our youth who are poised to create positive change. The **Book Release event**, a part of the **International Kindness Festival 2023**, is a unique opportunity for our youth to share a piece of their soul through the written word and/or artistic expression, and get their work published. Recognising that being comfortable with your authenticity is a superpower and a form of kindness to self.

ACKNOWLEDGEMENTS

Maya Thiagarajan – Founder, TREE Learning
Diana Shathish – Art Educator & Entrepreneur
Notion Press Publishing

Contents

Disclaimer *vii*

Introduction *ix*

1. Definition Of Friendship 1

Part 1

2. Small Moments 5

3. Reminders For You Today 6

Part 2

4. ODE TO ROSES 11

5. CURIOSITY: A Desire To Know And Learn 13

Part 3

6. Colours Of The Rainbow 17

7. My Heart Is A Library 19

8. Never Be Kids Again 20

Part 4

9. The Ripple Effect 23

10. Growing Up 24

11. Puzzle Pieces 26

12. At The End Of The Day 27

13. This One Goes Out To All The Girls And Women In The World 29

14. Polar Opposites 31

15. Magnets: Attract And Repel 32

16. Sabaism: The Worship Of Stars 33

17. Singing Again 34

18. Happy New Year 35

19. Thoughts 36

Contents

20. Creation 37

21. Truth: Shatter Some, Pickup Some 38

22. All The Reasons Why 39

Part 5

23. Silent Lovers 43

24. Things You Said Too Quietly 44

25. Birthday Balloons 46

26. They Told Me To Define Home 47

27. I Love You Or Whatever 48

28. I Can Set This World On Fire, And Call It Rain 49

29. A Warmth Of A Smile 50

Part 6

30. Broken Crayons Colour Just Fine 53

31. Heals The Broken And Lights The Brightest 54

32. Scars To Your Beautiful 55

33. Liquid Laughter 57

Part 7

34. Namma Chennai 61

35. Sensory Symphony 62

Disclaimer

All these poems are written with prompts that I have found scattered in small nooks and crannies, and all the illustrations used in the books were made by me.

Introduction

In life's beautiful chaos lies a home to a creative art called 'poetry'.

Welcome to the Rippling Effect. As you read this short compilation, you will delve into different scenarios, different time periods, different emotions, and different events in my life.

In this book, you will find verses tying friendship, love, different objects, phrases, and pieces of advice all together.

It doesn't matter if you are a poetry lover or someone who is just starting to discover this world. This book holds a place for you, and I guarantee you that you can hold any one (or more hopefully) of these poems with you.

As you read the poems, be prepared to be transported to different time periods and feel different emotions. Maybe even feel nostalgia or evoke or make memories.

Dear reader, I want you to step into a world of words and let the words come over you like waves.
I want to present to you the 'rippling effect' where poetry will let the world of imagination flow and the words guide you to unknown realms.
Have fun reading!

1. Definition of Friendship

I found the crumpled letter at the base of my school bag,
Found all the letters written,
crying, shaking, angry, anxious, happy,
Thought about all the times you ran behind me,
When I stormed away, when I ran away,
Felt the way your palms would rest on my shoulder,
When you needed to lean on someone when you were tired,
It made me remember, back to the first day we met,
They told me to define friendship,
One where there was an everlasting bond built from,
Trust, faith, hope, worries, secrets,
But also built from,
Queries, heartbreaks, fights, anger, hatred, jealousy,
They told me to define friendship,
Which one?
The toxic one, which always left me drained out,
Not satisfied, used, or
The safe one?
Which always left me charged,
Satisfied, respected, valued.
A symphony of laughter and tears,
Through the years, friendship flame shall forever abound.
With the empathy of the guiding star,
Two souls intertwine, no matter how far,

That's the definition of friendship to me.
It's a gift to be able to hold someone's heart
so dearly in your hands,
To trust in to protect, heal, nurture, and nourish.

2. Small Moments

We assume a perfect love story ends in marriage and creating your own family. What we don't know is that a perfect love story can also exist when you take a bite of your favourite ice cream, go on a magical holiday, play your favourite sport, listen to music that is a blessing to your ears, meet your favourite person after a long time, paint a stunning masterpiece, etc. If a perfect love story can end in various different ways, then why are our expectations of love always so high when we can love the small moments of our journey instead?

3. Reminders for you today

Reminders for you today
It's a blur of colours, people, emotions,
Places, seasons, time,
Words, images, imagination,
Often, we get told to stay in the moment,
To absorb, observe, reflect, embrace,
As I grew up, I understood why!
why they told me to be present,
Because all of this would just whizz past me,
I walk the streets of a crowded bazaar,
As I hear paisa dropping on scarred hands,
As smiles lit up their hopeful faces,
I was taught, being kind costs nothing,
I wrote a thank you note to my teacher,
I gave my seat up to a pregnant lady on a train,
I told this stranger that her outfit was beautiful,
I was also taught that expressing gratitude costs nothing.
Comparison, comparison, to what society thinks of each and every one of us,
To people we see online, to our friends, to our family,
I just don't understand why we put ourselves through those agonising thoughts,
It's like every day we run so fast, like we have to catch a train to different destinations,

Instead, I think we should all slow down, we are doing just fine,
Walking a path that God designed specifically for us (God is our helper; we design our own destiny)
Instead we should pour a little bit of love into everything we do,
Because I strongly believe that the kindness you put out in the world always has a way of coming back to you.
I refused to step foot outside when it was storming,
Because I let the fear of thunder take me over,
But eating the frog was a risky yet bold decision I took, which was worth it,
Sometimes, I let all the hatred in the world took over me,
As I had stormy clouds hang over my head,
I remembered that I had to talk to myself like I would talk to a loved one.
reminder: to love yourself and treat yourself with respect and kindness.
As I grew older, day by day, minute by minute, second by second,
This is what I learned.
Being kind costs nothing.
Slow down; you're doing fine,
Eat the frog,
Talk to yourself like you would talk to a loved one,
Stay in the moment.

4. ODE TO ROSES

It burns, it glows,
It breaks, it heals,
It repairs, it tears,
Red roses: love and romance
It inflicts, it stabs,
It blesses, it curses,
It is passive, it is active
Black roses: vengeance
It understands, it explains,
It interests, it fascinates,
It succeeds, it fails
Blue roses: mystery and intrigue
It loves, it hates,
It touches, it scratches,
It smiles, it cries
Pink roses: gratitude and appreciation
It purifies, it dirty's,
It cleanses, it triggers,
It nudges, it pokes
Purple roses: love at first sight
White roses: innocence and purity
It spreads, it collects
It radiates, it attracts
It bonds, it links,

Yellow roses: joy and friendship
Just a thought: do you see how all the roses balance each other in a bouquet?
That's how life is—a balance of all the different coloured roses, well! not all, but you get the idea. It's beautiful; let it stay;
don't change it.
We each have our own unique story to express and narrate, and I think that's amazing, elegant, and poised.
I personally love it.

5. CURIOSITY: A Desire to Know and Learn

Has one ever stopped to think about how infants touch and feel, listen and learn, see and grasp, or talk and register at the same time? Has anyone ever stopped to think about the way humans have evolved, the way our brains develop, and the way our alphabets string together to form words, eventually forming sentences? Has anyone stopped to think about how birds can fly, how trees dance around in the wind, how cars are powered by engines, or how spices enhance the flavour of a dish? This is just the bigger picture, but has someone ever really stopped to think about how the alphabet came about? Or how are the different parts of our brain used for different purposes? Or how many different species of birds and trees are there, and how do they adapt?

Curiosity fosters growth, which sometimes fosters innovation or change. Curiosity is good; I was taught that is the way we learn, as we ask questions and gather knowledge; sometimes that's the best and most efficient way to learn.

Eleanor Roosevelt once said: I think at a child's birth, if a mother could ask a fairy godmother to endow it with the most useful gift, that gift would be curiosity.

6. Colours of the Rainbow

We are all royalty,
With strong ambitions stemming from our hearts,
Every day we solve a mystery,
Violet.
Justice is such a common term,
Yet, does fairness guide the world?
Impartiality takes over,
Indigo.
Open fields filled with blue peas,
Shows the amount of freedom that exists,
Letting our imagination take the stage,
Blue.
We grow and mature with every passing minute,
In harmony we sing out loud,
Jealousy still exists,
Green.
The freshness of air floods the atmosphere ,
Stringing smiles on faces,
Energy sparks through every cell in my body,
Yellow.
Successful people start small,
Expressions spin stories,
Fascination is found everywhere,
Orange.

Sacrificed dreams,
Courage to step out,
Passion fuelling success.
Red.

VIBGYOR

7. My Heart is a Library

My heart is a library, it's not one filled with books, it's one filled with kindness, love and gratitude. My heart is a library filled with endless joyous memories of those who I love and those who love me.

My heart is a library, a path that is being navigated through the hard times and the easy times.

My heart is a library, a library where, in order to unlock every piece of treasure I hold, the right time, the right people, the right reason, the right situation, and the right tone are required.

Our hearts are a precious library, not only beating to keep our bodies alive but also bearing some of the deepest things we hold dear to us.

In my mind, everyone's heart is not something just keeping us alive; our hearts hold thoughts, feelings, emotions, and all types of relationships, but our hearts are special; they hold treasure worth a lot.

My heart is a library, filled with blood, veins, and arteries, translating to memories, bonds, and endless love.

My heart is a library.

8. Never Be Kids Again

In storybooks where dreams were laid,
In search of paths that life brought on.
Fake bills of youth, mere paper dreams,
Turned into truth by life's swift streams,
No longer play, but bills to pay,
Reality dawned, and colours turned grey.
Dream houses stood in skies so bright,
Yet time unveiled a different sight,
Harsh reality knocked on the door,
A humbling truth we can't ignore.
The pages turned, the chapters changed,
In winds of time, we rearranged,
From carefree hearts to cautious minds,
The journey's twists and subtle signs.
But 'midst the shifts and altering themes,
The essence of our childhood gleams,
In lessons learned and strength acquired,
In grown-up hearts, the child's desires.
For though the stories shifted pace,
And dream houses found a different space,
The spirit of those youthful days,
In who we are, forever stays.

9. The Ripple Effect

In a world where shadows often lurk,
An act of kindness, presents,
Like a water droplet touching the edge of a lake,
It is the love that sets ripples to make.
With a smile, a sentence,
Comes a chain of unplanned pleasure,
Kindness begets kindness; it's true,
Rippling, it touches not on but a few.
Just imagine a heart once filled with sorrow,
Light up by a spark light upon,
The heart beats with newfound grace,
Embracing another.
It's life's song, one we cannot meddle with,
Instead, we can play along to the tunes,
By altering or transposing,
A message of love, a selfless deed, echoes in a hope-starved world.
So let us remember the day we started.
This ripple effect is ever-so-strong,
To open our hearts and serve,
One act of kindness is all it is worth.

10. Growing up

This poem is inspired by a singer named Ruel and his song. This poem has some of his lyrics incorporated into it

Within the blink of an eye, we go from being dependent to independent,
Growing up is weird,
Sometimes we are mature, at times childish,
Sleep with friends, break hearts,
As we grow, our heart develops feelings our mind rejects,
We grab onto the first person we see, latching ourselves to them as if our existence is crafted around them,
Question everything you thought,
Was right, was wrong, question every single decision, thought, friendship, relationship,
Growing up is weird; fall in love for a year,
And then I disappear, wishing that you were here,
We end up feeling too hard, which is beautiful, but not for over-thinkers,
We merge into the shadows, hoping we sense comfort in them, or we emerge from the shadows stronger,
Growing up is strange,
Get too close and push away,
New regrets, new mistakes,
Every single day we have the choice to repeat or evolve. Some of us feel safe repeating, and a few feel safe evolving, but each day, each person, each action teaches us something.

Growing up is strange when the one who's to blame,
Is looking in the mirror a wish that you were here?
Sometimes we look back and think to ourselves what I will be, how different I could have been, or some of us think that we should have been more present in that moment before it slipped away, or some of us might think that life is moving too fast for me to catch up to speed with it.
Growing up is,
Strange,
Weird,
Scary,
Exciting,
Fun,
Yet growing up is a roller coaster.
Growing up is_______.

11. Puzzle Pieces

Cut at jagged edges, they still fit like a lock and key,
Piece by piece it builds a picture,
One that narrates, one that depicts, one that travels,
one that soars,
It's as though life's mosaic is being built out of fragments, fragments of
imagination, love, fantasy, reality, the future,
Its essence grows richer by the passing minute.
Together, they build, unveiling a grand collage,
Where dreams and memories interlock,
Capturing masterpieces of moments,
Coming all the way from dusty crevices to whispered visions,
In unity and in chaos, it orchestrates a symphony,
Puzzle pieces eventually find their own path, their own way,
Completing a grand design, that we call life.
Hand in hand the past and future dance, a mosaic of existence with every
glance,
So take a risk and let the puzzle pieces intertwine,
Creating something one of a kind.

12. At the End of the Day

At the end of the day,
A parallel motion guides the sky; the sun sets only to be replaced by the moon.
I look at all the stars twinkling, like a thousand diamonds,
At the end of the day,
I see lights light up buildings, cars honking as traffic builds up,
Filling up the bare stretches of tar and concrete,
At the end of the day,
I see tides rise aggressively and crashing on the shoreline,
I see crabs crawl into their respective holes built into houses,
At the end of the day,
I see people come back to their families after long hours of work,
Joy and laughter fill up the salty breeze as excited kids run around,
At the end of the day,
I hear birds chirp as they glide across the skies in a V shape,
Mothers tell their husbands and family to come home,
At the end of the day,
I hear church bells chime, and loud speakers recite prayers,
As everyone joins their hands or drop to their knees praying for various reasons,
At the end of the day,
I hear the busy bustling roads, alleyways die down,
As everyone is inside or asleep,
That's when an entire blanket of peace sweeps over, signalling the end of

another day.

13. This one goes out to all the girls and women in the world

To all the ones who are strong, to all the ones fighting silently,
To all the ones trying to be free, and to all the ones trying to seek help,
I don't care what background you come from or where you're from just,
Remember all the hurdles you have crossed,
Every two-faced path that you have encountered,
All the effort and hard work gone 25x8,
All the blood, sweat, and tears.
Whenever, wherever we will always be together,
You are a miracle; count every blessing, count every single way that you are lovely because you should praise yourself.
Praise the beautiful soul you have,
Praise the creative mind,
Praise your thoughts,
Praise your personality,
Praise every small little thing.
Many of us out there are models to many,
Spread the spark, light a match and spread flame,
Be bold, take those risks.
Because we women are stronger than people know.
It's a cheer

We are strong; we beige; we grow; we care; we nurture; we ignite; we follow; we chase.

Interpret this however you want, each brain thinks differently, different thoughts may spark up but that is what sets us apart.

And I like to think that is absolutely lovely.

14. Polar Opposites

If sunshine was a person,
They would brighten up someone's day,
If sunshine was a person,
They would radiate happiness,
If sunshine was a person,
They would spread light
Sunshine can feel like a hug for some people, a fresh start for some and a person for some.
If rain was a person,
They would be showering praises,
If rain was a person,
They would be cool,
If rain was a person,
They would be enemies for some and lovers for others,
Rain can feel like a blessing for some, an opportunity for some, and a person for some.
Nature never seems to fail us.
Polar opposites, huh?
But still, they form a cycle for survival: an ecosystem that thrives, new lives that flourish, and crops that grow, among many other things.

15. Magnets: Attract and Repel

For we are all magnets,
Attracted to the ones we love,
And repelled by the ones we hate.
You know how they say,
When we are with the right person, it heals.
When we are with the wrong person it wounds,
Smiles of all kinds, crawl up her face,
As she grits her teeth in some, as she relaxes her jaw in some,
It warms her heart, it sends shivers up her spine,
It calms her mind, it cleanses her soul.
You know how they always say,
Being with the right kind of people, Doesn't drain energy?
That person was her, she was that person.
Smiles, laughter, genuine happiness,
Joy, love, and warmth flooded her.
She attracted a few but repelled many.
Why can't we all be like her?
For we are all magnets,
Attracted to the ones we love,
And repelled by the ones we hate.

16. Sabaism: The Worship of Stars

Orion, Ursa major, Ursa minor, Aquarius, Leo, and Scorpion, to name a few.
Those twinkling diamonds in the night sky, dance around,
People pray, sing, write, stare in awe, in respect, in tears, in joy.
Thousands and thousands of miles away, they look upon us; they look over us.
Each speck reminds us of our hundred and one problems, but in the night sky, they all appear small.
They form constellations, bringing us together and drawing us closer to one another.
As people say, Sabaism is the word meaning worship of stars.

17. Singing Again

She took into account what the world described her to be; she modelled herself into a figure people liked, tried to be the bigger person, tried to blend in, and tried to put everyone else first. She lost her true self, melting into the words of everyone around her. Soon she realised that it was too late; she couldn't turn back, thinking about what people would say about her. There was always this burning question: how am I going to keep this fake image up? That's when she took the risk and decided that nothing mattered to her more than herself, so she changed because she wanted to; she found her rhythm again, her own beat, and started singing again.

18. Happy New Year

Bursts of colour float in the sky,
Load music plays from speakers,
Dance floor filled with blobs dancing around,
Stringed lights hang from the trees.
People celebrated their achievements this year,
The small wins and big defeats,
All the love and grief along the way,
Stopping and reflecting.
It's the season of celebration, holding onto the memories and lessons this year has given us. Moving onto the new year, with bigger dreams and clearer goals. It's the season of celebration and joy.

Happy New Year!

19. Thoughts

I thought we were all on the same level. We were all on the same page. Understanding and thinking alike Breathing and beating in unison. Bleeding blood onto pages, binding pages into books, books into series, and series into volumes Step by step, breathe by breathe, hand in hand, we inch forward. Expecting that we all think the same, breathe the same, and walk the same won't be possible, for we are our own selves; we are one in a million; we all can't blend in, and that's beautiful.

20. Creation

You know what the most beautiful process on planet Earth is?
It is creation,
We use facial expressions to communicate,
We use colours to paint a painting,
We use ingredients to cook a dish,
We use our body to dance,
We use our voice to express,
We use our words to write,
We use our minds to think, to innovate, to create.
We all can't create the same thing for we are unique, and that's what sets us apart.

21. Truth: shatter some, pickup some

T stands for traitor,
R stands for running,
U stands for unstable,
T stands for turncoat,
H stands for hurting,

Do you see how all of this is the opposite—truth, something so pure, fragile, and precious?
It could shatter some, leave some hanging, or pick up the pieces.
It is just a small, five-letter work with a deep, hidden meaning.
Truth is the foundation that builds all of us, our beating hearts guiding us, building trust, healthy relationships, and everlasting bonds. Truth is like laying bricks down to build a house; it is the start of a new chapter or adventure.

Elvis Presley once said, "The truth is like the sun. You can shut it out for a long time, but it ain't going away."

22. All the Reasons Why

All the reasons why.
All the reasons why I love you,
Why I adore you? Why do I look up to you?
Ask me all the reasons why, but not a single word will escape.
All the reasons why I can't say what I feel
Out loud, because of the fear and the scare,
All the reasons why I won't feel
Too fragile, afraid to be vulnerable, and used.
All the reasons why.
Question me on the reasons, but I will keep my mouth shut.
These days, judgement is a natural feeder for curiosity.
I have many reasons why.
The past, the present, and the future
The people, the emotions, the truth
Don't ask me to reason it out, because I won't; I refuse.

23. Silent lovers

In a world of diversity, we met, hearts entwined,
Silent lovers beneath the stars, our souls one,
Love at first sight, passing by in the night,
Two pairs of eyes look up and lock,
Worlds colliding, igniting a light,
Unspoken words spoke, in silence they swayed,
Passing love, passing by a shooting star,
Cherished moments slipping from sight,
A stolen romance, a connection felt in every second glance,
But loves not always fair,
Heartbreak a shadow, a burden to bear,
Shattered promises, disrayed emotions,
Silent tears whispered what words couldn't convey,
But let the world heal and mend,
Chivalry is not dead,
Love at first sight, glance is alive,
Rekindling a spark in hearts to be damaged to bear.
In silence, our stories will last,
Etching a mark into history I bear.

24. Things you said too quietly

The things you said too quietly,
The way you would whisper in my ear every time you wanted to communicate in a huge group,
The way you would convey sentences through your eyes in a manner that I would understand instantly,
The way you would start tugging on your necklace
Or playing with you earrings subtly sending me a sign of discomfort,
The way you would write lyrics instead of normally expressing them is to let me know what you were feeling.
These are some of the subtle things you told me too quietly. You taught me how to be bold, speak up, and vocalise, but instead you went into this cocoon.
The things you said too quietly,
The way you quieten down when we enter a room, but when we're alone, I know you're the life of the party,
The way you would hide in a corner when anyone approached you,
These are the things that spoke loudly to me; the things you said too quietly were the things that spoke to me the loudest.
Your eyes were like windows, revealing your untold tales,
You'd shoot a look my way, a language unknown yet known.
A code only we deciphered, there's no doubt.
Each word, a puzzle piece of what was in your heart,

The message came through clearly, even when words fell apart.
These were the things that painted our life's art,
Moments that spoke louder than words from the start.
"The Things You Said Too Quietly," a story that's ours,
Whispers in crowded spaces, love's hidden powers.

25. Birthday Balloons

you know I always assumed that birthdays were just something that kept coming around every year; but what I hadn't realised that for some people birthdays might illustrate milestones. Maybe on your first birthday, you starting spitting out gibberish and responding to sounds,
Maybe on your second birthday, you started following along with your eyes and recognising the faces of different people,
Maybe on your third birthday, you could start crawling fast and holding your own head upright.
Maybe on your fourth birthday, you could imitate sounds and start to play with your toys alone,
Maybe on your fifth birthday, you would be able to roll over on your tummy,
Maybe on your tenth birthday, you were able to create a wish list of everything you wanted,
Maybe on your twelfth birthday, you realised really how old you were and started living more,
Maybe on your sweet sixteen birthday, you realised how grateful you were for everyone and for everything in your life. I am still growing up, so I will know a lot about birthdays as I grow older, but I do know that when birthdays come, people sometimes have to celebrate without loved ones around; people might have to celebrate them all alone because people forget; people might throw a party for themselves; no birthday is the same for anyone; they all look different, I guarantee you.

26. They told me to define home

They told me to define home, a task hard,
It's not just 4 walls and a roof, it's where hearts are bound,
Where memories bloom, and love takes its form,
A haven from the storm, a tapestry of laughter and tears,
The echoes of dreams and whispered hopes with fears, A refuge, a harbour,
Where stars become candles, gleaming so bright,
Meals, a melody of grace,
Faces that welcome in every embrace.
Home isn't just a space; they told me to define it as a place where one lives permanently,
The chapters of life, in which our hearts believed,
A mural of moments, where love took the lead,
It's the echoes of childhood, a mother's lullaby,
A father's strong shoulder, beneath the open sky.
Home isn't just structure; it's the memories we hold,
In the warmth of its embrace, we find stories untold.
So, let them ask me to define home once more,
It's in the laughter and tears, the heart's open door.
Not just bricks and beams, but where spirits roam free,
Home is where you find yourself, and where you find me.

27. I love you or Whatever

In a world where words hold a lot of weight,
It's a feeling that's bigger than what words can convey,
I love you or maybe more is what I want to say.
It's not just a phrase, it's a promise so deep,
When we lock eyes and share a smile,
I love you or whatever maybe pans out a mile,
A treasure chest of emotions that can't be sold,
I love you or whatever comes to hold,
When words fall short, and actions don't act,
I love you or whatever, take a chat,
So let these words flow, like a river's shore,
"I love you," or maybe more, forevermore.
In the beauty of emotions, we truly discover,
That "I love you," or maybe more, is like no other.

28. I can set this world on fire, and call it Rain

Acts of service is where the heart lies,
I can set this world on fire, and pass it off as rain,
No one said I meant damage,
Instead, with the help of kindness, I will let sympathy lead.
Spark ignites with every action,
A light illuminating every dark night,
It will mend the broken, and heal the wounded,
With these acts, I will call the fire rain.
Softly spoken words of affirmation,
With love and caution,
Lift them higher,
And set this world ablaze.
In whispered wind, or open air,
My words echo,
Service to the world's needs,
I'll watch the flames of love engulf.
In each act of service,
Let the world know, you started a fire,
Words of affirmation, the heart longs,
I can set this world on fire, and call it rain.

29. A Warmth of a Smile

Warmth of smile, where connections reside,
Were words fail, but actions shine,
In the shape of lips, emotions share,
Depth of feeling, impossible to hide.
A language so innocent,
A soul finds its cure,
Speaks of joy in moments of sorrow,
A bridge between cracks.
Below surface levels,
Whirlpools may form,
Holding in the flames that light,
An art, widely used,
Holding a lifetime's worth of stories.
Love the smiles,
Give them and receive them,
For they are worth more than you know,
A true reflection of the human heart.

30. Broken crayons colour just fine

In this book called Life, we all have our own page,
With the help of broken crayons, we create our own stage.
Life's a canvas, with colours of different shades,
Don't fret when your crayons are not whole,
For beauty will still emerge from the depth of the soul.
Each little step you take is a colour making your world even brighter,
Broken crayons, colour just fine, my friend.
Embrace every moment, let your spirit unravel,
With each stroke of courage, your story will be told,
The broken crayon has its own beauty, and it's pretty.
Broken crayons they teach us design, teach us beauty,
For my friend, the broken crayons colour just fine.

31. Heals the broken and lights the brightest

In the depths of shadowed nights, where hearts are torn,
Kindness emerges like a star, its gentle light prevails.
It heals the wounded spirits, the broken souls it finds,
Igniting sparks of hope, in the minds of those.
The scars that mark our journeys, where pain has left its trace,
Are soothed by acts of tenderness, in this vast human space.
The gentle touch, a caring word, a gesture from the heart,
Can mend what's torn, make us reborn, give life a brand-new start.
In kindness, we discover strength
It shines upon our darkest fears, and makes everything feel right.
With every act of selflessness, with every heartfelt grace,
Kindness stirs a radiant fire, in each and every place.
So let us be the vessels, through which kindness finds its way,
Healing wounds, igniting hope, brightening each day.
For in the warmth of giving, in compassion's gentle flight,
We'll find that kindness heals the broken and lights the brightest light.

32. Scars to your beautiful

This poem is inspired by a singer named Alessia Cara and her song. This poem has some of her lyrics incorporated in it

She just wants to be, beautiful
But her soul is already crafted so pure,
She goes, unnoticed she knows, with no limits
But her worth is based on what others claim?
She craves, the attention she praises, an image
Yet she is a mess?
She prays to be, sculpted by the sculptor
Who is the sculptor? Societal expectations?
Oh, she don't see, the light that's shining
I wonder why? Maybe it is the noise?
Deeper than the eyes can find it
Can't you see how she is crafted?
Maybe we have made her blind
Self-conscious mind and identity?
So she tries to cover up her pain
Her strength lies layers deep,
And cut her woes away
'Cause cover girls don't cry
They learn how to fly instead,
After their face is made
The world should trade her heart,

But there's a hope that's waiting for you in the dark
You should know you're beautiful just the way you are
And you don't have to change a thing
The world could change its heart
No scars to your beautiful
We're stars and we're beautiful

33. Liquid Laughter

As tears fall from the sky,
In a focused manner, they multiply,
Pitter patter, pitter patter,
On surfaces, creating songs.
The earth quenches its thirst,
As the heavens above boom with light and sound,
Umbrellas come out, and puddles become playgrounds,
Let the raindrops fall, let us play,
For its rhythm, every problem finds a solution.

ORBIT
ORBIT

34. Namma Chennai

On the streets of Chennai, stories are told,
You see people practicing Silambam under the train station, boldly.
Metro work slowly takes over land, houses, and roads,
Traffic builds up haphazardly, throwing rules out the window,
Endangering innocent lives who have places to be,
Bridges become refuges for people passing by,
Cyclists, and motorists as the mighty power unleashes,
Fruit and vegetable vendors,
sit in lines with fresh produce,
hoping to sell to make their daily bread,
Chennai's streets so rich with culture,
Sarees of vibrant hues, a kaleidoscope of tradition,
Street food sizzling with elation, a true feast for the senses.
You see kolam lining peoples front doors,
Flower garlands hanging from houses, spreading cheer all around,
Peak into Chennai's streets,
Where paths may tread.
In the heart of the city is where stories spread,
Chennai's streets a vibrant ever changing crescent

35. Sensory symphony

In happiness, lies a symphony of senses,
It tastes like laughter, sweet as honey.
Each moment, a vibrant, flavourful delight,
A feast for the senses, a sensory flight.
Happiness feels like a warm embrace,
Soft as a breeze, a safe space.
It's the touch of sunlight on your skin so fair,
A gentle reminder that life's love is there.
Colors burst forth, in the day and night.
It smells like blooming flowers in the spring,
A fragrant dance, as joy takes to the wing.
Happiness sounds like laughter in the air,
It's the rustle of leaves in a calm, green glade,
Nature's soothing chorus, in serenade.
Happiness, a mosaic of senses combined,
A tapestry of joy, in heart and mind.
It's a treasure to cherish, a life's grand art,
A symphony of sensations, a love in every part.

www.ingramcontent.com/pod-product-compliance
Lightning Source LLC
LaVergne TN
LVHW021340160826
845679LV00008B/1420

* 9 7 9 8 8 9 1 8 6 4 8 3 2 *